anything

D0515615

Prehistoric Animals
SHARP-CLAWED
DINOSAURS

WINDMILL
BOOKS ™

New York

Published in 2015 by **Windmill Books**,
an Imprint of Rosen Publishing
29 East 21st Street, New York, NY 10010

Designed and illustrated *by* David West

Cataloging-in-Publication Data
West, David.
Sharp-clawed dinosaurs / by David West.
p. cm. — (Prehistoric animals)
Includes index.
ISBN 978-1-5081-9049-3 (pbk.)
ISBN 978-1-5081-9050-9 (6-pack)
ISBN 978-1-5081-9051-6 (library binding)
1. Dinosaurs — Juvenile literature.
I. West, David, 1956-. II. Title.
QE862.D5 W47 2016
567.9'1—d23

Manufactured in the United States of America

CPSIA Compliance Information: Batch #BW16PK: For Further Information contact Rosen Publishing, New York, New York at 1-800-237-9932

Contents

Austroraptor

AW-stroh-RAP-tor

Like all raptors, *Austroraptor* ran on two legs. It had a killing claw which it kept raised off the ground when it ran or walked. This claw was used to stab its **prey**.

Austroraptor was one of the largest raptors. Its long jaws were filled with sharp teeth which it may have used to grab fish from lakes and streams.

Austroraptor means "Southern Thief."

Austroraptor was about 16 feet (4.9 m) in length and weighed around 810 pounds (368 kg).

5

Deinonychus

dye-NON-ik-us

This active and agile **predator** hunted in packs. It attacked its prey by using its large stabbing claw while it held on with its clawed hands. Like many raptors its body was covered in feathers.

6

Deinonychus grew up to 9.8 feet (3 m) in length and weighed 130 pounds (59 kg).

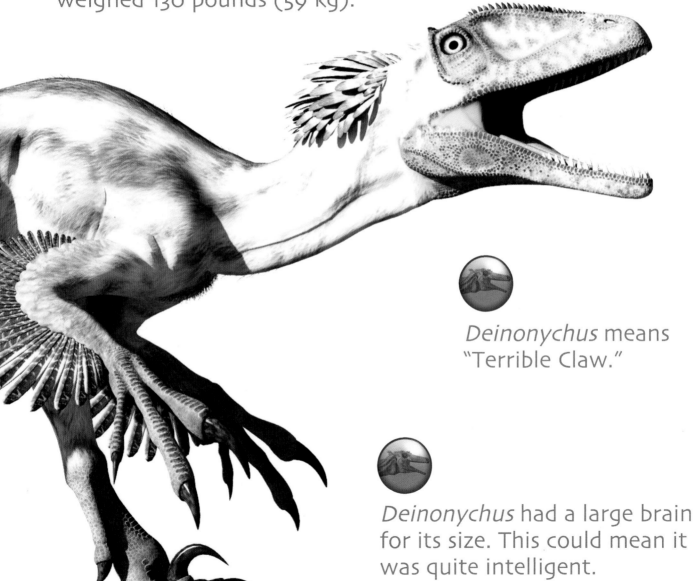

Deinonychus means "Terrible Claw."

Deinonychus had a large brain for its size. This could mean it was quite intelligent.

Gigantoraptor

gee-GIAN-tow-rap-tor

Gigantoraptor was not a true raptor. It was more closely related to the small *Oviraptor* (see pages 14–15). It was, though, a speedy hunter of enormous size.

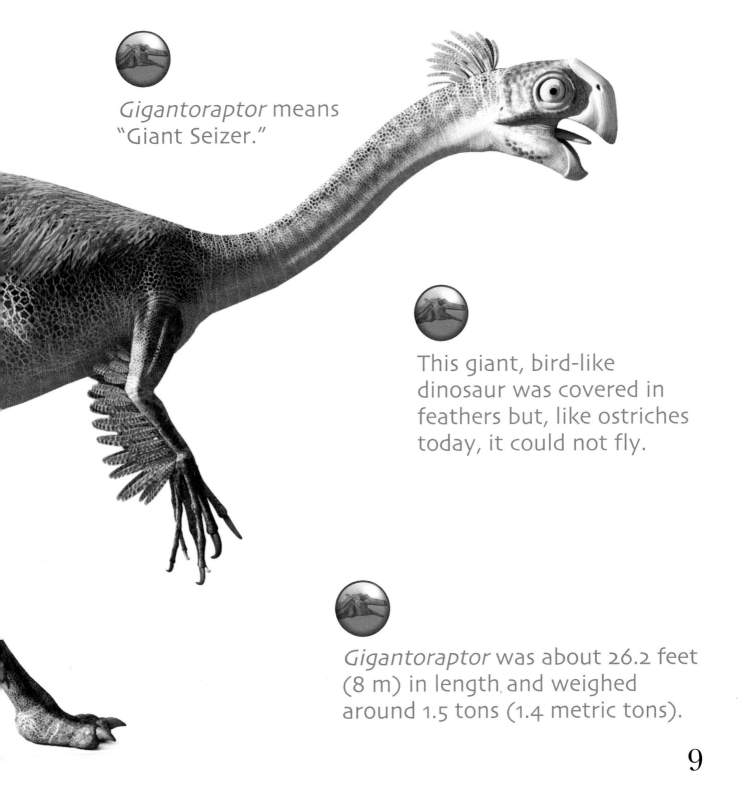

Gigantoraptor means "Giant Seizer."

This giant, bird-like dinosaur was covered in feathers but, like ostriches today, it could not fly.

Gigantoraptor was about 26.2 feet (8 m) in length and weighed around 1.5 tons (1.4 metric tons).

9

Microraptor

MY-crow-rap-tor

This tiny, feathered dinosaur had wing feathers on both its arms and its legs. Scientists think it spent most of its time in the trees. It glided from tree to tree looking for insects to eat.

Microraptor means "Small Thief."

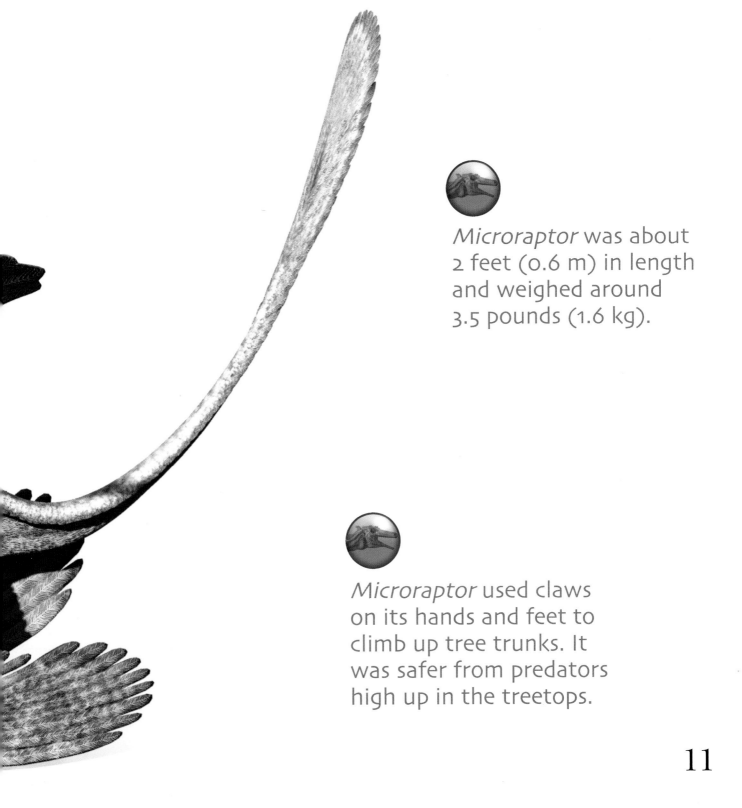

Microraptor was about 2 feet (0.6 m) in length and weighed around 3.5 pounds (1.6 kg).

Microraptor used claws on its hands and feet to climb up tree trunks. It was safer from predators high up in the treetops.

Mononykus

mo-NON-ih-kus

Mononykus was a speedy little dinosaur with long legs and short arms which ended in a single claw. It was covered in feathers which were used for warmth and display.

Mononykus means "One Claw."

Mononykus used its single curved claws to dig out insects from termite mounds.

Mononykus grew up to 5 feet (1.5 m) in length and weighed 10 pounds (4.5 kg).

Oviraptor means "Egg Thief."

Oviraptor was a meat eater and a **scavenger**, feeding on dead animals, clams, and even raiding nests for eggs.

14

Oviraptor

o-vih-RAP-tor

Oviraptor had an unusual appearance, very different from most dinosaurs. It had a bony crest and a strange-looking beak.

Oviraptor was about 7 feet (2.1 m) in length and weighed around 55 pounds (25 kg).

15

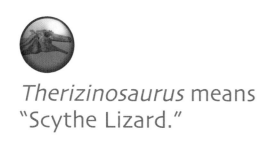

Therizinosaurus

thair-uh-ZEEN-uh-SAWR-us

This giant dinosaur had the biggest claws of all. Although they look like terrifying weapons scientists think they were used to drag overhead branches toward its mouth.

Therizinosaurus grew up to 26 feet (8 m) in length and weighed 4 tons (3.6 metric tons).

Therizinosaurus was a slow-moving plant eater. Its claws were just under 3.3 feet (1 m) in length. As well as helping it to feed, the claws might have been used to scare off predators.

17

Troodon grew up to 6.6 feet (2 m) in length and weighed 110 pounds (50 kg).

Troodon

TRO-uh-don

Troodon was one of the smartest dinosaurs. It was fast and had excellent vision so it might have hunted at night. It had large, killing claws on its feet, which were raised off the ground when running.

18

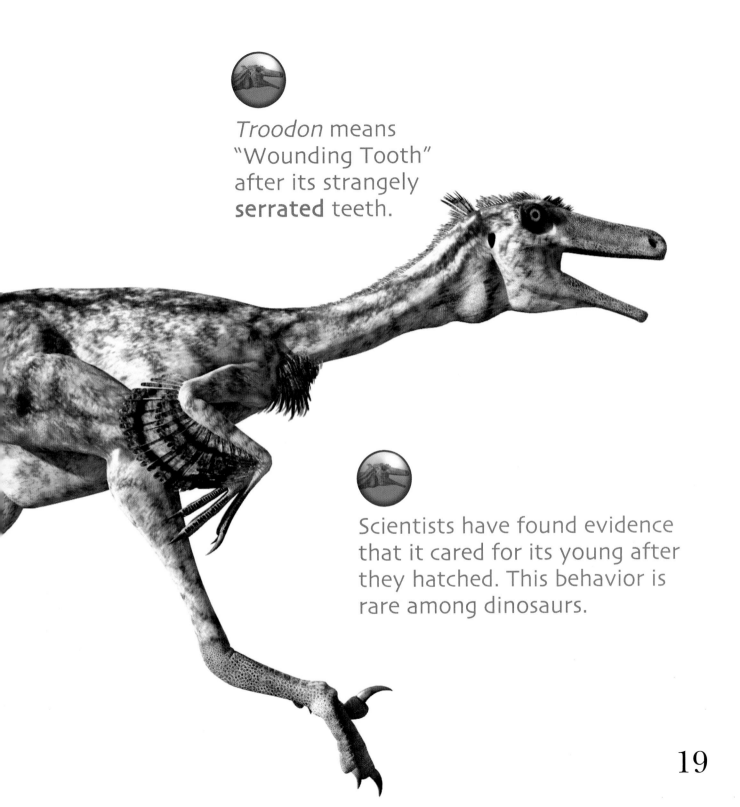

Troodon means "Wounding Tooth" after its strangely **serrated** teeth.

Scientists have found evidence that it cared for its young after they hatched. This behavior is rare among dinosaurs.

19

Utahraptor was the largest of all raptors. It is believed to have hunted in packs, which could mean it was an intelligent and warm-blooded animal.

Utahraptor

Yoo-tah-RAP-tor

This ferocious, speedy predator was armed with a 15-inch (38 cm) claw on one toe of each foot, claws on every finger of its hands, and razor-sharp teeth.

Utahraptor means "Utah's Predator" because it was found in Utah.

Utahraptor was 19.7 feet (6 m) in length and 1,540 pounds (700 kg) in weight.

21

It measured up to 5.9 feet (1.8 m) in length, and up to just 33 pounds (15 kg) in weight.

Hunting in packs, *Velociraptors* would have used tactics like lions do today to stalk and kill their prey.

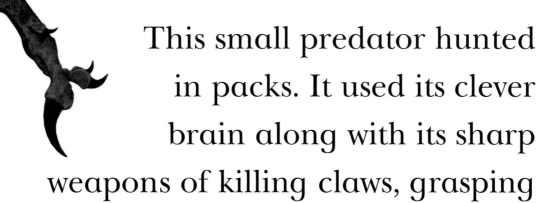

Velociraptor

veh-loss-ih-RAP-tor

This small predator hunted in packs. It used its clever brain along with its sharp weapons of killing claws, grasping hands, and needle-like teeth to bring down prey, often larger than itself.

23

Glossary

predator
An animal that hunts and kills other animals for food.

prey
An animal that is hunted by predators as food.

scavenger
An animal that feeds on dead matter.

serrated
A notched or saw-like edge.

Timeline

Dinosaurs lived during the Mesozoic Era, which is divided into three main periods.

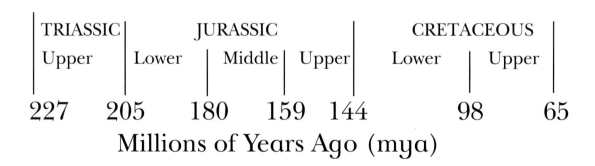

TRIASSIC	JURASSIC			CRETACEOUS	
Upper	Lower	Middle	Upper	Lower	Upper
227	205	180	159	144	98	65

Millions of Years Ago (mya)